# CHEER
## TOOLS
### AND GEAR

BY KRISTIN MARCINIAK

**CONTENT CONSULTANT**

**Pauline Zernott**
**Spirit Director and Coach**
**Louisiana State University**

**SportsZone**
An Imprint of Abdo Publishing | abdopublishing.com

ABDOPUBLISHING.COM

Published by Abdo Publishing, a division of ABDO, PO Box 398166, Minneapolis, Minnesota 55439. Copyright © 2016 by Abdo Consulting Group, Inc. International copyrights reserved in all countries. No part of this book may be reproduced in any form without written permission from the publisher. SportsZone™ is a trademark and logo of Abdo Publishing.

Printed in the United States of America, North Mankato, Minnesota
082015
012016

Cover Photo: Chris Williams/Icon Sportswire/AP Images
Interior Photos: Aspen Photo/Shutterstock Images, 4–5, 28; Aleksei Lazukov/ Shutterstock Images, 6; Greg Trott/AP Images, 7; Steven Senne/AP Images, 9; Conrad Poirier, 10–11; Richard Paul Kane/Shutterstock Images, 13; Shutterstock Images, 14–15, 18; Seppo Sirkka/EPA/Newscom, 16; Xi Xin Xing/iStockphoto, 17; Corey Perrine/ Naples Daily News/AP Images, 19 (top); iStockphoto, 19 (bottom); Derrick Tuskan/Icon Sportswire, 20–21; Richard Lewis/Icon Sportswire, 22–23; Sergey Minaev/iStockphoto/ Thinkstock, 24; Everett Collection/Shutterstock Images, 26; Megan Maloy Image Source/Newscom, 27

Editor: Mirella Miller
Series Designer: Maggie Villaume

Library of Congress Control Number: 2015945864

Cataloging-in-Publication Data

Marciniak, Kristin.
 Cheer tools and gear / Kristin Marciniak.
  p. cm. -- (Cheerleading)
 ISBN 978-1-62403-983-6 (lib. bdg.)
 Includes bibliographical references and index.
 1. Cheerleading--Juvenile literature.   I. Title.
 791.6/4--dc23

                                                  2015945864

# CONTENTS

**CHAPTER ONE**
THE RIGHT GEAR
FOR THE JOB
4

**CHAPTER TWO**
CHEER UNIFORMS
10

**CHAPTER THREE**
CHEER STYLE
14

**CHAPTER FOUR**
PROPS AND TOOLS
22

GLOSSARY 30
FOR MORE INFORMATION 31
INDEX 32
ABOUT THE AUTHOR 32

# ONE
# THE RIGHT GEAR
## FOR THE JOB

Cheerleaders are athletes. They push their bodies to the limit as they leap, dance, and tumble. Their gear is designed to keep them safe during practices and performances.

Some cheerleaders cheer for school sports teams. They lead fans in chants and cheers. Some school cheerleading teams also go to cheer competitions. Teams compete in front of judges and large crowds.

Some cheerleaders cheer on recreation league teams. Recreation leagues are for kids who want to play sports outside of school. Recreation cheerleaders cheer for athletes in the league. Recreation cheerleaders can also enter competitions.

College cheerleaders prepare to get the fans excited.

A group
of Russian
cheerleaders
perform at
a competition.

Professional cheerleaders do not have stunts in their routines.

All-star cheerleaders focus on competitions. They are known for their high-energy routines and spectacular stunts.

Professional cheerleaders entertain crowds at professional football and basketball games. Their polished routines are more dancing than cheering.

## FOLLOWING THE RULES

Each type of cheer squad follows a different set of rules. These rules cover everything from stunts to skirt length.

Recreational cheer squads do not have a specific set of rules. Professional cheerleading squads do not have a governing body either. They each set their own rules. Most cheer competitions follow rules set by the American Association of Cheerleading Coaches and Administrators (AACCA) and the US All Star Federation (USASF). They may also have additional rules of their own.

## ONE TEAM, ONE LOOK

Cheer gear varies by team. Some teams need uniforms for cold weather. Others need outfits that allow them to do handsprings. Every person on the squad wears the uniform. Shirts, skirts, and shoes must match. No single person should stand out. This shows that the squad works as a team.

A common look is also important in competitions. Judges look for a neat appearance by the entire squad. A team with mismatched outfits looks sloppy. Sloppiness distracts viewers from the performance.

Many cheer teams also have uniforms to wear in cold weather.

# TWO

# CHEER UNIFORMS

Cheerleading uniforms have changed over the years. College cheerleaders in the 1920s wore long skirts, sweaters, and tennis shoes. The uniforms changed as cheering became more athletic. Skirts were shortened and became formfitting. Many pieces of today's uniforms are made of spandex, which allows the body to easily move and stretch.

## TOPS

A cheerleader's outfit starts with the shell. Shells can have short sleeves, long sleeves, or no sleeves. In colder weather, cheerleaders wear bodysuits under their shells. Bodysuits are thin leotards with long sleeves. They keep muscles warm.

Stunts and jumps in the early 1900s were not as difficult as they are now.

## THE COST OF CHEER

Cheerleading can be an expensive activity. Every cheerleader needs a uniform, shoes, and pom-poms. There are also warm-up outfits, cheer bags, cheer accessories, and, for some squads, summer cheer camp. All-star cheerleaders have extra costs. They pay for gym memberships, competitions, and travel. All-star cheerleaders can spend up to $5,000 each year.

## BOTTOMS

Almost all female cheerleaders wear skirts instead of shorts or pants. Skirts are very short for safety reasons. Too much fabric can be dangerous when doing stunts. It can tangle around the legs or flip into the eyes.

Cheer briefs are worn under skirts. They look similar to underwear or bike shorts. Some squads put their team name or logo on the seat of their briefs. Others wear briefs with animal prints or fun patterns.

Shoes are an important part of the cheer uniform. Cheerleaders who tumble a lot need lightweight shoes. Cheerleaders who do a lot of stunts should have shoes with flat soles and sides that are easy to grip. All cheer shoes should have good support in the sole and ankle to prevent injuries.

Uniforms are designed with safety in mind.

# THREE

# CHEER STYLE

A cheer squad's style or look sends a message to audiences and judges. No matter how a team decides to style itself, everyone on the squad must match. Audiences and judges notice everything about a squad's appearance.

## HAIR

In the 1970s, most cheerleaders wore their hair loose and flowing. In the 1980s, teased and curled hair was popular. Some teams do not allow long, loose locks. It can be hard to tumble and dance with hair flying everywhere. Loose hair also can look messy by the end of a routine.

When everyone looks the same, it is easier for viewers to focus on the performance.

Wearing your hair in a ponytail means you'll be able to see better while you perform.

Today's squads typically wear their hair in high ponytails for games and competitions. This keeps hair away from the face. It also ensures that everyone on the team looks the same. A squad member with short hair may not be able to wear her hair in a ponytail. That is okay. She can use barrettes, elastic bands, or a nonslip headband to keep her hair out of her face. Hair accessories should be made of cloth or rubber. Metal clips or parts can hurt you or a teammate if a stunt or flip goes wrong.

A girl with shorter hair can clip it away from her face.

# BOWS AND MAKEUP

School and recreation squads wear bows with their team colors.

The most common cheerleading hair accessory is the hair bow. Hair bows come in all shapes and sizes. Flashy makeup can also be distracting. After a challenging routine or a hot day on the field, makeup will end up smeared and messy.

It is not usually recommended for young cheerleaders to wear a lot of makeup.

All-star squads might choose bows with sequins, glitter, or rhinestones.

Most older cheerleaders use heavy makeup so the audience can see it.

Cheerleading experts recommend that middle school cheerleaders skip wearing makeup. High school cheerleaders, on the other hand, are expected to wear light, natural-looking makeup, such as lip gloss and mascara. It gives a professional, polished look that shows the squad's dedication to the fans and the teams they support.

All-star makeup can be more dramatic. Some squads wear brightly colored eye shadow or lipstick to coordinate with their uniforms. College and professional cheerleaders also wear heavier makeup. They use products that last a long time, such as waterproof mascara.

Jewelry is usually not allowed for cheerleaders of any age. It can be dangerous. Even the smallest earrings can cause an injury if stunts do not go as planned.

## PERFORMANCE NECESSITIES

Cheerleaders carry their gear in matching cheer bags. Cheer bags hold everything you need for cheering, such as uniforms, shoes, and pom-poms. Many cheerleaders also carry accessories, makeup, hairbrushes, hairspray, and water bottles in their bags. Some even carry extra socks and briefs in case a team member forgets theirs.

# FOUR

# PROPS
## AND TOOLS

Cheering is a physical activity. Cheerleaders use their voices, hands, and bodies to get the crowd excited. But it can be hard to capture the attention of a big crowd. That is when props are useful. Some school and recreation squads use props to help them become more visible on the sidelines. All-star squads use props to interact with their audience.

Props should be lightweight. They should also be easy to hold, especially if they are used in pyramids or other partner stunts.

College cheerleaders use megaphones to call out chants.

## POM-POMS

Pom-poms are strips of vinyl gathered into fluffy balls. When shaken, the strips flutter in the air, making a rustling sound. They come in different sizes and lengths.

Pom-poms are available in every color of the rainbow. Most squads select their school or team colors. Poms with metallic finishes are common. They add extra sparkle and shine to a squad's routine.

Poms are used in pairs, one for each hand. Some have handles, which make them easy to hold during cheer routines. Others have elastic straps that go around the wrist or the hand.

Some cheerleading teams use different colored pom-poms.

Cheerleaders have been using megaphones since the early 1900s.

## SIGNS AND MEGAPHONES

The sounds of a big, excited crowd can drown out the voices of cheerleaders. That is when cheer teams use signs. Signs tell the crowd what to chant. Most signs have one word, such as "Go!," "Fight!," or "Win!" A cheerleader holds the sign above his or her head when it is time for the audience to shout that word.

A megaphone is similar to a microphone, but it does not use electricity. Its cone shape magnifies the volume of a speaker's voice. Voices are made of sound waves. When a person speaks normally, sound waves travel in every direction. But when you shout, "Go, team!" into a megaphone, the sound waves are trapped inside the cone. They are funneled in one direction, making your voice sound louder.

**FIGHT**

Signs are used to encourage the crowd to yell.

27

## FLAGS AND BANNERS

Flags and banners are used a lot by college and high school cheerleaders at sporting events. Flags are made of nylon fabric. Words, letters, and team logos are sewn onto them. Similar to signs, flags and banners are used to get the crowd excited. They are usually larger than cheer signs. They are mounted on long poles. Squad members hold the poles so the flags wave high in the air. Several flags can be flown in a row to spell a word, such as "L-I-O-N-S." A large flag might have a team's name and mascot.

Cheer props help cheerleaders spread spirit to the very last row of the bleachers. Like a team's uniform and style choices, they help communicate the squad's dedication to their performance.

Usually cheerleaders run around the field so the whole crowd can read the flags.

# GLOSSARY

**COMPETITION**
The process of trying to win something that someone else is also trying to win.

**COORDINATE**
To work together smoothly.

**LEAGUE**
A group of sports teams that play against each other.

**LEOTARD**
A tight-fitting piece of clothing that covers the torso and sometimes the arms.

**PROP**
An object used by a performer to create a desired effect.

**SPIRIT**
Enthusiastic loyalty for an athletic team.

**SQUAD**
A small group doing the same activity, often a physical activity.

**UNIFORM**
An outfit that all members of a group wear in order to match.

# FOR MORE INFORMATION

## BOOKS

Farina, Christine, and Courtney A. Clark. *The Complete Guide to Cheerleading: All the Tips, Tricks, and Inspiration*. Minneapolis, MN: MVP, 2011.

Webb, Margaret. *Pump It Up Cheerleading*. New York: Crabtree, 2012.

Webber, Rebecca. *Varsity's Ultimate Guide to Cheerleading*. New York: Little, 2014.

## WEBSITES

To learn more about Cheerleading, visit **booklinks.abdopublishing.com**. These links are routinely monitored and updated to provide the most current information available.

# INDEX

AACCA, 8

all-star cheerleaders, 7, 12, 21, 22

banners, 29

bodysuits, 10

briefs, 12, 21

cheer bags, 12, 21

competitions, 4, 7, 8, 12, 16

cost, 12

flags, 29

hair, 14, 16, 18

hair bows, 18

Herkimer, Lawrence, 25

jewelry, 21

judges, 4, 8, 14

makeup, 18, 21

megaphones, 26

pom-poms, 12, 21, 25

professional cheerleaders, 7, 8, 21

recreation cheerleaders, 4, 8, 22

rules, 7, 8

shells, 10

shoes, 8, 10, 12, 21

signs, 26, 29

skirts, 7, 8, 10, 12

USASF, 8

## ABOUT THE AUTHOR

Kristin Marciniak is a graduate of the University of Missouri School of Journalism. She has researched and written more than a dozen books for grade schoolers. Raised in Bettendorf, Iowa, Marciniak lives in Kansas City, Missouri, with her husband, son, and a very friendly golden retriever.